We are all destined for a journey
that will not only change our
lives, but the trajectory of
everything we thought could
be possible. I hope you take
that first step into your life soon.

-karnes-

The Black Journal

-A Poet's Journey-

1:54PM
10.25.23
Texas

Bring me back to where it
all went wrong. Back to where
you left me with my soul in my
throat. Only then will I be able
to devour the light again.

1:53PM
10.26.23
Texas

When my mind becomes a place
of war and death, I close my eyes,
and remember what you said
when you told me, "I will love
you on days when all you feel
are moments of fleeting,
moments of fear."

1:56PM
10.26.23
Texas

I must become a better version
of who I thought I would
already be by now.
Everything we need is
all but a breath and
moment away.

1:58PM
10.26.23
Texas

Take my hand and I will
embrace your worries.
We have always been
the same. My darkness,
your light Your darkness,
my run to. We are not
here to save one another.
Only our love matters
and guides our souls.

11:26AM
10.28.23
Texas

We are the dreams walking,
　　the truth shaking trees,

and a love story far from being
　　over. A story for our

own lives. You are enough on
　　your own. I hope one

day you believe it to be true as
　　much as I believe in

your touch keeping the flames
　　from my face.

12:49PM
10.28.23
Texas

.I wish I would have found love
for myself sooner, but whenever

it finds you, you will

forget what they did to you and
how they

left you where you thought you

were not enough.

9:29AM
11.4.23
Texas

There may never be another time
to do what you

love. You will never be this age,
this version

of yourself, and this health.
Take advantage

of it all while you can.
You are not any

randomly made storm. You are

the perfect storm.

9:42PM
11.4.23
Texas

Take your time with the love
for yourself.

Each morning, take the deepest
breath you

can. Each morning, hold yourself
accountable

for your actions. Show your
soul gratitude

and grace. It is experiencing
you and all your

happenings for the first time in
this lifetime.

10:16AM
11.4.23
Texas

Be sure you are living the life
you promised yourself
when you were a kid in your
room. When all you knew
how to do was survive until the
next time you felt safe.
We are more than the weight of
the burdens we harbor.
We are humans who deserve
love, and nothing but the
greatest love there is out there
for the scars we had to
become to remember why we
bled in the first place.

1:00PM
11.6.23
Texas

Today is my dad's birthday.
Number seventy for him.
It is almost hard to believe he
is this age. You never
appreciate the time and day
until your parents begin
to hit these pivotal years.
You never realize how
quickly they go from raising
you to growing old with
you, until you are older than
they were when they
were once trying their best to
love you as a child.

Happy Birthday, Dad. I love you.

9:11AM
11.11.23
Texas

Give into the love, the peace,
and the ability to
see yourself as you are.
The mirror does not
reflect the soul, but a soul
we are, and a soul
we will give hope to when
all things have
faded from darkness, out to
the edges of
every dying star calling us
by name.

9:19AM
11.18.23
Texas

I do not know if we will ever
meet or hold the
other, but this pause is not out
of hesitation.
It is me being unsure of where
you came from
and what you see in me that
makes you
want to be here alongside me,
keeping all
of the walls from closing in
on me.

10:45AM
11.18.23
Texas

I know you may never be
ready for anything
more than my shadow next
to you, but if you
are ever in need of more,
take my hand, for it
has held the mountains who
were afraid of heights.

3:13PM
11.22.23
Athens, TX

My grandmother would do anything for anyone. All she knows is love and how to give love. A precious human with an angelic soul. No one else could ever be her. No one could ever replicate the light she pours into the day and night. She'd make you forget how much of your life had gone wrong and tell you how you are right where you need to be. She would show you how to survive after losing your significant other, and turn death into a dedication to live your life for them, instead of waiting on your turn to go.

9:47AM
11.23.23
Athens, TX

Happy Thanksgiving.

I am thankful for my family,
my health, and my work.

To be great, you must know what
it is to fail. Being this

way, you must proceed in
excellence, knowing it does

not exist in this world as we
know it.

9:54AM
11.26.23
Athens, TX

Drink your coffee. Be thankful
for the weather,

family, and experience you are
getting here.

Everything comes and goes,
but you can

make the day as long as you
need.

9:56AM
11.26.23
Athens, TX

Mornings like this, I imagine
your coffee cup next to

mine, your hand reaching for
mine, squeezing with a

need to be closer than the light
resting on your lips.

10:04AM
11.26.23
Athens, TX

I look at you in the morning,
before the

sunlight reaches its hands over
the mountains.

I take in your smile, your eyes,
and the way

you move slightly to the right.
Your grin is

full of every possibility. I am
in awe of

how you breathe, star child.

8:06AM
12.2.23
Texas

Be where you need to be
mentally, physically,

and spiritually. We cannot
allow someone else
to dictate how we view
love, ourselves,

and our worth. Some people
love the game. It is
why they smile behind your
back when you are

laying flat, wishing they would
talk you down.

8:08AM
12.2.23
Texas

I am sorry and apologise to
myself for thinking

someone meant what they said
when feelings were

involved. Humans can never
properly share how

they feel until they show you
who they are first.

11:49AM
12.10.23
Texas

I am constantly learning how to
adjust to the light.

My eyes are full of memories
both from what the

dark and shadows have created.
I am getting

closer to the sun, but never far
from the twilight.

1:33PM
12.15.23
Texas

If you do not take time
for yourself, you will

never see the shimmer
your flowers are in

need of. You will
never see how the water

runs down your face,
when all you need is to be

reminded of how to cry
when your chest begins

caving in from holding
in what you need to
let go of.

9:30AM
12.17.23
Texas

Tell me how you feel. Tell me

where it hurts the most. Tell me
the secret you keep in the pages,

and I will write how much you
are loved. I will write out

where you can rest as I lay my
hand on my shoulder and chest

after I am through with
whispering to you, you are loved,
you are needed, you are enough.

9:55AM
12.17.23
Texas

You may feel unworthy today of
the blessings in

your life, but you tend to forget
the amount of

times you fought for others
without fighting for

your own life. The universe sees
it all. It gives

back more than you ever could.
How do you think the moon got
to where she is tonight?

10:02AM
12.17.23
Texas

There is beauty in the suffering.
If it were true,

these flowers would not need
more light and

rain. I am tired of suffering.
I need more than

this fear of being unloved.
I need to close my ears to the
mouths that only are fed
by cowards and devils.

5:13PM
12.22.23
Boerne, TX

As the years go by, learn how to
appreciate the drive all

the more when the location is no
longer to your

grandmother's house. Thirty plus
years goes by in a blink of an eye
if you are not ready for the
change. One day, there will

be nowhere to go or anyone to
hand the presents you once
bought those you loved.

We pay a full price when it
comes to what time can steal.

8:44AM
12.23.23
Boerne, TX

Morning light grazes the trees,
awakening the dead

leaves to give more breath to the
humans walking

underneath. The magic is in the
admissible surviving,

the prominent impermanence.

3:23PM
12.24.23
Boerne, TX

A full house, presents, tree,
family, food and
every personality under one
roof, is the sound of
meaning. Once a year,
everyone returns to being
a kid, wearing their pajamas,
and waiting on
Santa. The only difference is,
you get to see
how life once was for the
parents who became
the elves to make sure you
had everything you
asked for when times were
difficult for everyone.

10:27AM
12.26.23
Boerne, TX

I do not know what the new year
will bring, but I

am hopeful the change we all
need will be found

in the effort we put into the last
few days and

how much we put into the year
that sits here,

waiting to die for another to
be reborn.

4:02PM
12.26.23
Texas

Back home after the holiday
being with family is

always a mixed bag. Depleted of
energy, but my

ideas, and dreams are full.
New Year on the

horizon. It always feels like
more needs to be

done, then you will have time
to sit and rest.

2:24PM
12.27.23
Texas

Take these bones and make a
man out of me,

a human where death once lived.
I will help

you gather the flowers for the
eyes you

tell me no longer see beauty.
Lead me to the grave you have
designated for yourself,

and I will lead you back to the
place where love outlasts
everything death believes it
can touch.

2:30PM
12.27.23
Texas

My unhappiness taught me how
to endure the

struggle without dragging others
into the misery.

Life is our choice, as is our smile
that can

represent the pain or joy from the
day. We all must suffer

one of these days. Loosen your
grip. Unclench your fist.

Pain can make us monsters if we
let it, but it can also create a new
page for us to begin on.

2:31PM
12.27.23
Texas

Your situation has nothing to
do with me.

You chose your life before you
met me. I can

only do so much when you were
the one

who wanted to leave me in the
first place. Save me the story
of you missing me. I told
you that you'd

regret it, and here you are now,
making my life more
complicated than I can have it.

1:40PM
12.28.23
Texas

I am still learning my needs,
my wants,

my expectations for my own life
and what

that looks like going into the new
year. I will

speak every single thing into
existence. I will

not get in my own way. I will
prevail with a victory.

1:23PM
12.29.23
Texas

We will never get the change we
are after until

we change the situation we are in.
Living in the

energy around you will always
dictate the

environment you either thrive in
or survive in.

9:16AM
12.30.23
Texas

Drink your coffee. Sugar, milk,
cream, or black.

Watch your thoughts in the
morning. Speak to

someone, everyone, or no one at
all. Our finish

line is all the same. Enjoy the
sunshine and hope

of finding more beauty to write
about, to exist

with until you permanently have
it in your life.

11:58AM
12.31.23
Texas

HAPPY NEW YEAR'S EVE!!

May today be the jumping off
point for you.

May it be the last day you ever
feel you

need to look back to see where
you are going.

NEVER

BEFORE

SEEN

WRITINGS

All were typed or

handwritten never to be

shared, but with new books,

come new meanings behind

the reasons why you wrote

them in the first place.

I hope you enjoy their

addition to the book.

8:03PM
5.28.19
Mesa, AZ
Country Inn & Suites
#431

May you travel often and find
yourself marrying
every moment you make.
When the sky gets tired
and the sun goes down,
those colors, those feelings,
they are all saved from a
day many held onto so they
would know what they had
and made it beautiful.
The light only enhances our
hearts and what our souls look
like under a roof of magic.

4:59PM
5.28.19
Mesa, AZ
Country Inn & Suites
#431

Love is something that is out
there, and I am too out of

touch with reality to have it now.
It exists within

the confines and outlines of
everyone who

makes you fucking feel
something. We are never

without it. We are just without
those to speak it to.

5:54PM
5.28.19
Mesa, AZ
Country Inn & Suites
#431

You deserve someone who is not me. Someone who is not a recovering addict. Someone who is not still trying to love himself after all of the failures. Someone who is not trying to hide his face in the stars to get away from the man he is. You should never have to worry about anything or anyone who is not yourself. You will always look and feel familiar to me. You will always be too good for anyone because I know who you are. I knew I could not keep you. As much as it hurts, I know you will find someone who is not me, and I will smile when you do. You gave me the best years of my life, and that is is more than anyone has ever given me. When someone asks me what happened, I will look for you, and tell them, "She did."

5:22PM
5.28.19
Mesa, AZ
Country Inn & Suites
#431

My branches may be shedding
their leaves, but they

will fall with a meaning, with a
truth, with an undying

love to never fully touch the
ground until you can

catch me and hold me for a little
while before I get

back up on my feet, and go on
without you again.

12:52PM
5.26.23
St. George, UT

I had a dream last night where
I needed you and
you turned away. It went on until
I woke up.
It's funny how much of our
dreams mirror reality
when we actually remember
them. The silence does
not hurt anymore. I know there is
healing within the
pain. I know where you cannot
be for me, I will be
for myself. I am having to learn
how to love once
more in this life of mine without
anyone to return it
back to me the way I give
without being asked to.

12.29PM
5.26.23
St. George, UT

I travel to know the moon better,
to know her every side, phase,
and feeling she exudes. There
will never be a time in my life
when I am not trying to be closer
to her. Closer to her, is as close
to anything real I will ever have
in my life. Distance is a number
made up to keep doubt fresh in
our minds. No obstacle will keep
me from being one with her light.
No death could ever kill the soul
and keep her out of my grasp, in
full. No one could ever change
my mind about who it is that
changes the smile on the moon.

12.24PM
5.26.23
St. George, UT

I sit here and think about you.
It is what I am best at these days.
It is all I know. A heart cannot
erase a love that has made a
dream become true. Time cannot
forget what life does to the world.
You will always be my best
friend. Even during our absence
from each other. Even if we
never talk again. I know too
much about you for my mind to
ever think of someone else the
way I still adore you. I know too
much about you to ever forget
any of it in order to get to know
someone else in this lifetime.

10:31AM
4.3.24
Texas

There will come a time when
you will feel as though
you have given enough of
yourself to the place you
are at. When you feel that pull
to seek out more,
I hope you take the sun and
moon with you for
as long as they give you their
light. Life is too
short to play it small, without
chances taken for the life and
love you deserve.

Only be afraid of never being
yourself. The rest of
your life needs the next
version now.

12:17pm
5.31.19
St. George, UT

We are the lonely ones, a single
dream away from awakening

our own reality. There is light
in you that needs

to breathe. Let it in. Let it out.
Give it away. Give it all to your
next adventure. Give it to the
human you are

trying to find within your own
failures and shortcomings.

Whatever you decide to do
next, take your own hand
and lead for once.

2:45PM   2.19.21   Texas

I am not happy. I have not been happy in quite some time. I think it is important we speak openly about how it is we feel even if it is not what we or anyone else wants to hear. Honesty has been with me since my mother took me into her arms and told me she would do her best raising my brothers and I after the divorce. Transparency was learned through observing others living their lives in full, without shade or shadow blocking out who they really were. I have been a million different faces and whatever emotion was needed at the time to survive. I am the furthest thing from sainthood, but I am closer to my own beliefs than most are. If I cannot be myself on here or with those in my life, I am not doing anyone justice. I am simply folding myself in-half, in quarters, to fit into whatever narrative others need. I am not afraid to talk about how I feel, because once you die a few times, there are no words that can be said to you that can impact how you live your life afterwards. The absence of happiness in my journey has nothing to do with love or missing someone or missing out on something. It has everything to do with me not being able to be present where I am. It stems from knowing this is not where I want to be, all the while losing days, months, and years to a feeling I cannot give credence to based on my location currently. When you are born a wanderer, a journeyman, life takes on an entirely different meaning. It is about raking in the sunshine and taking in the moonlight as often as possible from differentiating places. It is about meeting strangers and discussing life and finding out who they are. It is about fulfilling a promise you made to your younger self to take pride in what you do and shedding who you have had to be in order to get here. It is reconnecting to the light you have been seeking since darkness raised you. Being an empath, you know a calling when you feel it. The last three years, I have not felt anything besides loss. Being unhappy is a choice in a lot of ways. Patience is a skill you cannot barter to attain. My priority is finding good in everything in hopes of it leading me to where I belong. For now, I will continue to dissect myself in front of the class, in front of everyone to see how far this pain actually runs inside of me. It is the only way I know how to write my poetry in the manner of truth. To know yourself means to know the reasons as to why you suffer or have suffered. It is to know who you are when the love is gone and you are left by yourself in an empty room, with all your belongings packed up and hauled away. You must sit with yourself to understand the stories of your life, and how often they get misconstrued by the path we take for a better ending. There is nothing wrong with you if you feel lost and abandoned. The best humans have had to sift through their own wreckage to find the gold they thought others had stolen.

1:05PM   7.27.24   Texas

Where I sit, the sun smirks with

sadness hiding behind its gleam.

To know the moon so intimately

and be this far separated at the

same time, causes the light to

break things it should never

touch at all.

1:43PM 7.31.24 Texas

You are the bond between soul and flesh. You are never an afterthought, because no one can pull the tides like you. No one could ever orchestrate the rise and fall of every moon that has ever lived and breathed before. Do not diminish yourself or your powers based on the inabilities of others to love and show you they mean it for the first time.

6:39AM   4.27.22   SL TX

As the light breaks wide open,
you should know that my hope
is to be yours by morning.
My dream bleeds in color,
hoping to find your body
somewhere close to wherever it
is my bones feel most at home.
I believe in truth and yours is my
favorite texture and placement.

6:57PM   7.11.23   RM334

May there always be a sound of goodness within your actions. Not a look. Not a movement. Simply a light to you which remembers. Simply a light to you which reverberates and vibrates the darkness others may find themselves in. Be content when a fullness finds you. There is no reason to give gluttony a seat beside the meal. We are all experiencing life. Be kind, and smile when you feel the moment. Love with all you have fought for, and it will fight back for you in a fullness only reserved for kings and queens.

7:43 AM   8.2.24   Texas

It is there that I will learn how to keep the moon in your eyes and flowers in your words. I know how it feels for someone to look you in the eyes and promise they will never leave, then leave without a trace. I will not give up on you, because you could have given up on me, but you stayed. Even my last breath will have you and the moon entangled inside of it. As soon as her eyes light up about anything she loves, a thousand books are already written. I am grateful there are no such things as coincidences when it comes to someone loving you, because they have loved your soul before this life gave you a face to be recognized by them at the right time.

www.ingramcontent.com/pod-product-compliance
Lightning Source LLC
Chambersburg PA
CBHW021810130726
47987CB00010B/3096